HER LIGHT
The Journey Toward Becoming

DEFYING THE ODDS AND MOVING WITH PURPOSE

BRITTANY CUTTS

Print ISBN: 978-1-63616-202-7
eBook ISBN: 978-1-63616-199-0

Published By Opportune Independent Publishing Co.
www.opportunepublishing.com

Printed in the United States of America

For permission requests, please email the publisher with the subject line as "Attention: Permissions Coordinator" to the email address below:

Info@Opportunepublishing.com

Contents

Dedication

To my parents, so much of who I am today is from what you instilled in me at an early age. I appreciate you both for empowering me and letting me know that with God, all things are possible. You both also demonstrated the meaning of hard work and perseverance. You have been my biggest cheerleaders, always encouraging me to be the best that I could be and to shine brightly in all things. There aren't enough words to communicate my appreciation. However, if I could sum it up in two words, I'd say: Thank you.

HER LIGHT

Preface

When the thought was placed on writing a book, I was initially very reluctant. I couldn't fathom the thought of being vulnerable to an audience and sharing my story on a public platform in this way. Many things crossed my mind, such as: What will people think? How will it land? Will it have an impact? I then tapped into the spiritual reason as to why I was writing it: Because God said so.

Whenever I have been obedient to His word, I have always found clarity in the storm. The journey of writing this book began in 2022 when I was going through a difficult time. I began journaling my experiences and feelings, and as pieces gathered together, I started to see the light in the storm. *HER LIGHT: The Journey Toward Becoming* is meant to be a tool that inspires readers to keep pushing through life's trials and tribulations and make it to the other side of purpose.

Father God,

I want to start by saying thank You. Thank You for my journey; thank You for my story that is unique and special to me. I thank You for everything that has shaped me to become who I am today. Thank You for allowing me to reach the point of living a purpose-filled life, in which I pray that I can be a beacon of light to those in need. I pray that those reading this understand that their story is still being written; I pray for a realization that the wounds of their past have made them warriors and that the journey is maneuvering them to higher heights even when they can't see it. My prayer for those reading this is to know that there is so much to be thankful for, and with You, all things are possible. I pray for every soul to see the light at the end of the tunnel and to keep moving toward greatness.

In Jesus' name,
Amen.

CHAPTER I

Foundation

Throughout the years, I have grown to understand that there's a multitude of things that contribute to the makeup of a person. There's, of course, the obvious: genetics. However, as you dive deeper, you realize that a person's upbringing and childhood experiences, religious beliefs, cultural exposure, trauma, relationships, etc. all add to the makeup of who someone is. For me, it began on a warm summer day in the '90s, as I was born in my native Grand Rapids, Michigan.

I was brought into this world and grew up with two loving parents and an older brother. My mom is a southern girl who was raised in Tupelo, Mississippi, and grew up as the youngest of seven. On the contrary, my dad was born and raised in Grand Rapids, Michigan, and he was the youngest of four. When it comes to my brother, five years separate us in age. I am very grateful to have grown up with both of my parents. One thing that I can stand certain of is that if it was not for the sacrifices that they made for us and the strength that they displayed when we experienced the most adversity, I don't know where I would be today.

To describe my parents, my mom is very gentle, nurturing, optimistic, giving, and warm. My dad, very outgoing (some would say talkative—if you know, you know), hardworking, and very expressive. They both grew up in the church, and my father became a minister in his teen years. When it came down to their religious beliefs, they were consistent in their individual and joint Christian teachings with me and my brother. My faith has always played a big part in who I am.

We were the family that grew up going to church every Sunday, and when I say every Sunday, I mean *every Sunday*. That meant that even when we went out of town, my dad made sure to find the nearest church to go worship at. Growing up as a "PK" (preacher's kid) was not always easy. In my early years, I have so many memories of going to gospel quartet concerts, gospel workshops, revivals, and programs. So, it's safe to say that quite a bit of my early years was spent in worship settings.

On top of that, my family was well known in the church community. On my dad's side, my grandmother, two aunts, and uncle all became ordained ministers. They also were heavily involved in the music industry; they had a group called the Wings of Faith Juniors, which originated when my father was just the mere age of five years old. My dad was one of the lead singers along with my aunts, and my uncle was known as one of the greatest lead guitar players in the city. Even as the group stopped performing, my dad remained persistent with bringing in artists, MCing, and putting on gospel concerts for the community. Whenever I'd watch my dad in his element, I'd see something light up in him.

Though this was my upbringing, I personally didn't know what it was like to have a true relationship with God. That was not developed until a much later time in my life. Often feeling like I was in the spotlight, I felt like I had to display a certain level of perfection. I feared making mistakes and being judged for a very long time. This quickly developed into becoming a massive people pleaser and someone who sought validation from others prior to making decisions.

The funny thing is, despite the self-inflicted pressure that

I felt, I never experienced those pressures from my parents.

NEVER WOULD HAVE MADE IT

When thinking about high school, so many memories come to mind. It's such a delicate time in your life. Friendships are strengthened or broken by the various cliques around school, feeling the pressure from consistently hearing, "What are your plans after high school?" Oh, then there's the first loves and high school romances. When I entered high school, I experienced all of that. I met great people, and I also lost some friends. I had puppy love, then I experienced my first heartbreak. I also pondered the endless possibilities of what I wanted to do after completing my four years of high school. However, what ended up happening from my ninth- to tenth-grade years is not something that I could have planned for. Within a year, my maternal grandmother passed away, my aunt died of cancer, and my family and I experienced the scary and devastating loss of our home due to arson from a racial hate crime.

Yeah, you read that right. Talk about an overwhelming time in my life. The feelings of grief sunk in, though I didn't even know at the time what I was experiencing. The loss of loved ones, as well as the loss of my childhood home, scarred me for many years. When it came to the racial hate crime, my family and I were thankfully away from our home; however, my parents received a call during the early hours of the morning telling them to rush back home. I recall the street being flooded with cop cars and state troopers because whoever did it not only spray-painted racial slurs on the side of our home and our African American neighbors' homes, but they also painted a threatening message about our president at the time, Barack Obama. We gathered what we could, but I recall bawling as my childhood memories were tarnished. All pictures had now vanished, and I was saddened by the fact that someone could do something so mischievous to people based on the color of their skin.

Up until that point, I'd only seen my dad cry two other times in my life: when my grandfather and aunt passed, and now, a third time after losing our home. I can only imagine the stress and agony that my parents experienced as they tried to figure out what was next for me and my brother. To this day, the one thing that I'll never forget is my brother's comfort. As I sat weeping and fearful, I remember him giving me a hug and saying the simple words, "Brittany, don't cry. Everything is going to be okay." Despite how things appeared, I believed him. How my parents responded next is what began to really put an imprint on the shaping of my character and how to respond in moments of despair. That Sunday, my dad got up and told us all to get dressed for church. Despite losing material things, we had so much to be grateful for, and we still stood together as a unit and family. My parents showed me that we may have been knocked down, but we were going to get back up and keep moving forward. My brother's pastor at the time preached a well-needed sermon, and the community came together and helped my family out immensely.

In that moment, I learned how to pray and fight to keep going despite how circumstances may have seemed. The firm foundation that my parents had established for us allowed me to have hope and faith. For the next month, we stayed in a hotel until the apartment was ready to go. It was the wintertime, so finding a readily available apartment near my school for a family of four and a dog was not easy to come by. Many would think it was a vacation to essentially live in a hotel, but we ate out so much that the thought of fast food started to disgust me. For the next six months, as we transitioned to getting adjusted to living in our apartment, I listened to two songs nearly every day.

Those songs were "Never Would Have Made It" by Marvin Sapp, and "Let Go" by DeWayne Woods. The lyrics that resonated with me were:

"I'm stronger; I'm wiser; I'm better, much better. When I look back over all You brought me through, I can see that You were the one I held on to." — Marvin Sapp

"There's so much goin' on. Sometimes I can't find my way, and oftentimes I struggle. Struggle from day to day. I have to realize that it's not my battle; it's not my battle to fight. I have to know if I put it in Your hands that everything will be all right." — DeWayne Woods

To me, these lyrics taught me that though trials and tribulations may come, you are stronger than you may realize, and the situation will make you wiser and better. It also taught me that everyone goes through a journey in life, and we all experience difficult battles that we have to fight. However, once you stop worrying and put your problems in His hands—or, as I commonly heard growing up, "give it to God"—everything will be okay.

Throughout the time that we'd lost our home, I was also a cheerleader at my high school. One of the biggest competitions of the year was approaching. That year, the cheer program made the decision to donate some of the proceeds to my family. After seeing the overall compassion that my team showed me, that's when I developed a true love for cheer. It pushed me to want to show the same compassion and be the person to lift others up because it was done for me in a big way. One of my favorite scriptures is Romans 8:28 NIV. It states, "And we know that in all things God works for the good of those who love Him, who have been called according to His purpose." The acts of kindness from others as well as watching my parents' strength and resilience helped me to flip a switch. It was the most defining moment of my life. I realized that I had a choice: Be bitter and sulk in everything that we'd lost, or find a way to see the good in the situation.

What I went through that year established such a humbleness in me. As I got older and began to tell my story, I'd often be asked things like, "How did what you went through not cause a dislike for people who didn't look like you?" I'd learned that despite my experience, I could not allow myself to get to a point of disliking others or treating them poorly based on what I'd gone through. I'd grown to realize during that season that though the time was tough, I had people believing in me, praying for me, caring for me, and showing immense amounts of love. I'd think of great leaders such as MLK who'd experienced great extents of racism; instead of hatred, he'd shown love, and that's the approach that I took. Throughout that journey, the switch that flipped was that I began finding who I was throughout the pain. I'd started becoming someone who eventually leaned toward taking an optimistic approach in life and using that as a token to help and inspire others. Many years ago, that led to a point in time when I'd written down a statement. It stated, "I will always work hard in everything that I do; I will not back down when obstacles are thrown my way; and I will change my attitude, be humble, and always find something to be thankful for."

CHAPTER 2

Got Spirit?

We got spirit! Yeah, yeah, we got spirit! Yeah, yeah! We got the what-what-what-what-what-what-what-what-what-what-what? We got spirit!

I can't tell you how many times I'd heard the words of that chant growing up. There's no hiding that my time cheering and coaching had one of the greatest impacts on my life. The first time that I took an interest in cheer was when I was eight years old, and my dad signed me up for a youth program in the freshman campus where I'd eventually end up attending school. As my dad was formerly a boxer, he always told me that he wanted to make sure I could defend myself. So, naturally, when looking at the list of activities that I could sign up for, karate was at the top of his list. One thing that I can say about karate is that though my stint in the sport was short, the tools that I learned during that timeframe stayed with me. I remember going to practice, and as we practiced in the main gym, the cheerleaders had the top portion of the gym above the bleachers. I could often hear their competition music, and I got so drawn in by their fancy uniforms, shiny pom-poms, and hair bows. I remember begging my mom to let me drop out of karate and become a cheerleader, which I eventually did.

As I moved on to middle school, my parents really wanted

to ensure that I had the opportunity to focus on the transition of leaving elementary school. Therefore, I didn't participate in sports at my school until the following year, seventh grade. I was a very active kid in middle school; I wanted to do it all and try it all. I was an honor roll student, and between my seventh- and eighth-grade years, I'd also been part of musicals, played tennis and volleyball, ran track, and, of course, cheered. Though I loved cheer, I also really enjoyed theater and volleyball.

Now, the middle school that I went to was also the middle school that my brother attended. Back in his day, he was well known in school due to his musical abilities, as well as sports. He played basketball and wrestled. Since the coaches, who were also educators at the school, took a liking to my brother, they'd naturally done the same with me as his younger sister who also attended the school several years later. As eighth grade was coming to an end, and as teachers and counselors were actively trying to help prepare students for the transition to high school, I recall having a conversation with my assistant principal. To this day, I am appreciative of that brief conversation with him. He'd known me and my family for quite some time, as he was also formerly my brother's coach. Due to the conflict in when these activities occurred throughout the year, I had some decisions to make. I was torn between playing volleyball and participating in theater or cheering for our high school's football team as well as going out for competitive cheer. During my conversation with him, he emphasized how he'd seen me light up when I cheered and how he felt that was the route that I should go, and I listened. Talk about a defining moment—a brief conversation with someone who I trusted impacted the trajectory of years to come.

My first two years of high school, I cheered on the sidelines for the football team and for the competitive cheerleading team. Here I was, at a D1 school, cheering for a program that had made it to state finals at the time for the last five-plus years. I was so amazed that I'd even made junior varsity (JV) as a freshman. In that moment, I was thinking, *Man, my assistant principal was right.* I'd made the right choice. As my junior year approached and the program conducted sideline cheer tryouts in the spring, I'd said, *Okay. This is my moment. I'm going to work my butt off at tryouts, and I'm going to do all that I can to shine.* I knew I didn't have all the gymnastics skills that the varsity team typically looked at, but I said that I would try my best. At the end of tryouts, coaches would have everyone sit on the gym floor, thank us for trying out, then call our names as they handed out letters informing us of who'd made the team and who hadn't. As they called my name, my stomach sank and my heart began racing as I walked up to grab my letter. Up until this point, I was MVP multiple times over the last few years of my cheer career, but there was a thought in the back of my head that it could all be ending in this moment.

I'd heard multiple squeals from those who also got their letters and found out that they'd made the team, and I'd also seen several girls burst into tears or who were angry that they hadn't. Now, it was my turn to find out. I took a gulp and a deep breath as I slowly tore open the letter addressed to me. I saw a big whopping *Congratulations* at the top of the letter, and it included details of what to expect over the summer and upcoming season. I was ecstatic! Here I was, being able to continue my journey with cheer on a prominent team in our city.

Shortly after I opened my letter, a bomb dropped. The three varsity coaches, as well as my now former JV coach, approached me. My big smile slowly faded away as they shared some news with me. They said that my gymnastics and stunting skills weren't strong enough, and I originally was not going to make the team. The reason that I'd ended up making it was because my JV coach fought tooth and nail for me. She'd believed in me and informed them how they would be making a mistake by not putting me on their team due to my work ethic, my leadership, and the energy that I brought to the seasons when she was my coach. What they told me was that they would use the upcoming summer as more of a probationary period, and they gave me a timeframe for when they wanted to see my skills improve, which was by the end of August.

I first looked at my JV coach in a way of appreciation for her belief in me. At that moment, I knew that I couldn't let her down, and I was just so thankful that she saw something in me at the time and used her platform and voice to speak up for me in rooms that I wasn't even in. That gesture became another defining moment for me when it came to doing the same for other people, which I will share later. I thanked my new coaches, and I knew that it was time to get to work.

THE PROCESS

Going from previous seasons in which I was a leader and top performer on the team to now being questioned and often feeling like I didn't even deserve a spot on my new team was not an easy adjustment. However, I began forming a "prove it" mindset. I was going to prove it to my new coaches, I was going to prove it to my new teammates, I was going to prove it to my JV coach, and most importantly, I was going to prove to myself that I could do it. That summer, I became super obsessed with my personal growth. I worked out consistently, I built up my strength and endurance, I went to open gyms nearly weekly for gymnastics, I partnered with my teammates outside of practices to help spot me on tumbling skills, and I'd done it all with an optimistic attitude.

August came, the timeframe that my coaches had given me for when they wanted me to have the necessary skills for the first game. Not only did I get the skills that we'd talked about months beforehand, but I'd also surpassed my goal. One of my coaches pulled me to the side and let me know how proud of me she was and just how much I brought to the team. I finally felt like I could breathe. I'd done it, and I had also proven to myself that with consistency and hard work, anything is possible. I was proud of how far I'd come and the tenacity that I had to not give up.

The season came to an end, and the competitive season was quickly approaching. Now, mind you, I thought it was hard to make the sideline team—I'd heard that it was *way* harder to make the competitive team. I'd pondered on the thought time and time again whether to go to tryouts or not. I'd built a bond with my team, and I'd grown an even deeper love for the sport. My coaches had gotten past teams to state finals consecutively for the last several years, and this year, we just knew that this specific team really could take the win. As the time for tryouts quickly approached, I made the decision not to attend. I sat in my room, saddened by the fact that I would not be continuing to another season. However, I'd gotten to the point of being afraid of rejection. Despite my efforts and progress over the past several months, imposter syndrome crept in. I couldn't fathom the thought of my coaches coming up to me again and breaking similar news. All I kept thinking was, *I'm not good enough, I'm not going to make it, competition is too high, and I'm just not going to try.* Up until this point, I'd rarely been a person to speak things like that about myself.

The next day, I connected with several of my cheer friends, and they discussed how tryouts went. I remember it like it was yesterday: I arrived at my Spanish 3 class, and my teacher let me know that my coach was on the phone. She was also a teacher at the school. I walked up to the desk and answered the phone. My coach let me know that she was very surprised that I did not attend tryouts. I was transparent in letting her know my worries and that I thought I just wasn't good enough to be on the team. She said something along the lines of, "Just because someone isn't the quarterback of a football team doesn't mean that they aren't a valuable member of the team." Her words landed with me, and I made the decision to attend day two of tryouts. After the third day, I'd made the team, and I knew it was go time.

In Michigan, competitive cheer consisted of three rounds. The first round focuses on jumps, ripples, and motions. The second round focuses on a 10-count precision drill, unison of motions, and gymnastics skills. Lastly, round three focuses heavily on tumbling and stunting. I competed in round one that year. To this day, it's one of my favorite rounds to watch in Michigan competitive cheer due to athletes' creativity and their ability to draw in the judges and crowd. Whenever I would perform, the adrenaline took over from the moment someone set the cheer. My thoughts were, It's *showtime*. I beamed with facials portraying my confidence on the mat, and I made it my priority to always at least get a smile from the judges. I eventually ended up becoming front and center that year.

We had a stellar season. The year prior, my high school was runner-up, so we just knew that we had to pull the win this go around. That season, we were conference and district champs. However, though we had seen much success, our coaches always humbled us and let us know that we had to work for what we wanted and nothing would be handed to us. We knew that leading up to districts, if we wanted another week together, we had to fight for it. As we moved on from districts and regionals and made it to state finals, my adrenaline was at an all-time high. Here we were performing at an arena full of people. Back in those days, teams didn't have assigned sections for their schools, so you'd literally see fans camped out or there at super early times of the morning just to secure a prime parent and student section for their school. The lights were beaming brightly, and there were cameras everywhere. As they called my team for round one and we set the cheer to begin, once again, it was showtime.

We performed all three rounds beautifully. As all the teams swarmed to the mat to see who would be crowned this year's champions, we gripped each other's hands in hopes for the news that we'd wanted. As they got down to the remaining teams, we got more and more excited about not hearing our name yet. Many teams formed themes for their season that went like this, "Our name called last," indicating that they planned to take home the victory. That was our goal, as well, and that's the mindset that we had—until our name wasn't called last. We got third place that year by an excruciating number—half a point. By less than a point, we went from first place to third place. When you break down how small of a number that is, a fraction of the performance that we'd given justified our first-place victory becoming a third-place loss. It was more painful knowing that we were that close to winning rather than losing by a wide range.

IMPACT

Senior year, I competed in additional rounds. During the off season, I took a similar approach as I'd done the year before, and this time, I focused heavily on becoming stronger and on my technique as a base. I'd reached the point of being able to fly any flyer on our team, which is something that I was proud of. Though we didn't reach our goal of becoming state champions that year either, I was able to walk away thankful that I'd found something that I was truly passionate about, and I also learned a lot about myself.

While cheering, I truly learned the meaning of hard work

and dedication. I learned not to quit just because things were difficult. Shortly after graduation, I became a coach myself, and I went on to coach for nearly six years. It was not until I became a coach that I truly grew an appreciation for my own high school coaches. The difficult decisions and sacrifices that they had to make, building the morale of the team, and inspiring those around them, all while creating a competitive yet humble team culture, was truly admirable.

There was such irony in me becoming a coach. I went from almost not making the team my junior year in high school to having the opportunity to coach over 150 girls as well as become an MHSAA judge over the course of my coaching career. I coached a variety of age groups—middle school, junior varsity, and varsity—and hosted kids' camps, which included kids as young as six years old. It was a joy working with kids of this age and seeing the teams step into leadership opportunities. One of my fondest memories is a picture that was taken of the kids admiring the athletes in what is called a liberty. It went to show that you never know who is looking up to you, literally, so use every opportunity that you get to be a leader and inspire those around you. Despite the countless positive memories and heartwarming moments, I want to be transparent in discussing some of the difficulties in my coaching experiences because they created so much of who I am today. Particularly, my first two years as a varsity coach pushed me and brought out a side of me that I didn't know I had. I saw so much of myself in many of the girls that I coached, and my priority was less about winning or losing and more about pouring into the team, providing opportunities that they didn't think were possible for them, and letting them know that they had someone who believed in them.

I'm the first to admit that I did indeed struggle when it came to adjusting to coaching, especially when it came to creating some sort of balance for myself due to the busyness of my work, school, and cheer schedule. My last couple of years of coaching were tough, and I was mentally exhausted most days. However, I'd truly created a "fake it till you make it" mindset. Most days would look like this: I would wake up at 5 a.m. and complete any remaining assignments that I did not finish the night prior. I would then head to work and get there by 7:30 a.m. At the company I worked at during that time, my shift was from 7:30 a.m. to 6 p.m., and I knew that if I didn't leave work by 6:07 p.m. at the latest, I would be late to practice. I then conducted practice from 6:30 p.m. to 8:30 p.m., and I would make it home around 9 p.m. From there, I would eat dinner and work on any assignments due for the week, oftentimes up until 11 p.m. or midnight, as I was also a full-time student. Not to mention, if it was a competition week, this often threw my schedule out of whack even more depending on whether it was a weeknight competition or a big Saturday competition. I also struggled as I was in my early twenties and navigating through developing as a young adult. Personally, I experienced difficulties when it came to creating boundaries with parents and, at times, allowing the pressure and criticism to get to me. It trickled down to my athletes as well. I was truly a people pleaser and often operated that way as opposed to being consistent, remaining firm, and operating how I truly wanted out of fear of being disliked.

I always made sure that I was present with my team. They often laughed because I always had some sort of reminder on my phone going off during practice to ensure that I would not miss a deadline or follow-up pertaining to something cheer-related. I did my best to create opportunities for my athletes, whether that was being on the news, practicing with college coaches and teams, performing halftime at basketball games, or gaining community exposure. As I look back and reflect on my time coaching, though I had challenges, I would never take back my experiences. Graduating from college was one of my proudest moments. For me, it meant more because it was far from easy. You see, my athletes fueled me to keep going and see the light at the end of the tunnel. All those late nights and early mornings studying and completing assignments, I kept telling myself that I could not give up. I wanted to show my girls that even though times were difficult, the season of difficulty was only temporary, and even if that meant slowing down or reprioritizing certain areas in their lives they could accomplish anything that they set their minds to. In high school, we had an unspoken rule of, "Check it at the door." That meant that when you made it to practice, it was important to do your best and bring the best version of yourself. This personally helped to establish an optimistic attitude that formed so much of who I am today and the energy that I brought to my own teams to encourage them to take an optimistic approach to life. I am also thankful for every opportunity that I had to pour into the team. I would often recall the moment that I had with my JV coach when I was sixteen years old; her belief in me created a belief in myself. I made it a priority to do the same because you never know who you can impact.

CHAPTER 3

L.O.V.E.

I remember the first time that I heard the song "L.O.V.E." sung by the famous Nat King Cole in one of my favorite childhood movies, *The Parent Trap.*

L — is for the way you look at me
O — is for the only one I see
V — is very, very extraordinary
E — is even more than anyone that you adore

That movie, and countless others that had that song as a part of their soundtracks, seemed so magical; it highlighted such a beautiful moment between a couple falling in love. Growing up, I, like countless other little girls, dreamt about meeting my prince, and I imagined what my wedding would be like. I envisioned what my cake would look like, what style my bridesmaids' dresses would be, having my dad walk me down the aisle, how my hair would look, and the list went on. When it came to my future husband, I never had an image of what I thought the person would look like, but I always wanted someone who valued me and honored marriage according to God's vision.

In my twenties, I had few long-term relationships. My dating experiences leading up to 2019 were not the best, but one thing that I am appreciative of is the fact that I learned something from each one. In the fall of 2019, I met someone, and after about two months of dating, we made things official. There was something about this guy that I could not put my finger on. He was charming, outgoing with a contagious personality, and warm; he had a strong faith, poured into me with positivity, and the list went on. Though there were naturally areas for improvement, the good qualities quickly outweighed them.

The massive outbreak that took over everyone's lives called COVID-19 quickly happened about six months into us dating. Throughout that time, due to the isolation, we spent quite a bit of time together and fell in love, and nearly a year and a half later, he proposed to me. He did so on my twenty-seventh birthday, surrounded by my family and friends. I said yes! I could not believe it—the moment I had dreamt of for so long was finally happening! I had just gotten engaged! Now, it was time to prepare for the wedding. I'd set up pre-marital counseling and began thinking of who I wanted on my side, and he did the same for his groomsmen. We established a budget and I began looking for my wedding dress and all the joyous (and stressful) things that come with planning a wedding.

Like many people, throughout the week of the wedding, I had wedding day jitters. I was making such a huge, life-changing decision this week. I was nervous, excited, anxious, and so many other feelings mixed all in one. On the day before the wedding, the stress and pressure of our approaching wedding got to us. We had a huge argument, and throughout our dispute, I really began questioning if I wanted to proceed with getting married. I'd spoken to several people and walked through my concerns; I'd pulled out my laptop and drafted an email to send to everyone letting them know that the wedding was called off. After calming down and being reassured by the individuals whom I had confided in, I realized that I probably was overreacting. I was extremely exhausted, and I thought it was all getting to me and my judgment. Besides, I had 180 guests arriving the next day and many people flying in, we had already crossed the refundable portion for food and drinks, the reservation of the event space was nonrefundable, and the list goes on. I asked myself, *Is it worth throwing away thousands of dollars and financially impacting those who are coming, as well as the money the wedding party has already spent? More importantly, is it worth potentially risking my fiancé not wanting to go along with my plan of taking more time with each other and truly deciding if we're making the right decision, all due to a hunch that could be wrong?* So, I had convinced myself that I was, once again, overthinking, as I tended to do, and we proceeded with everything as planned the next morning.

The wedding was gorgeous, from the event space to the floral arrangements to the wedding party to the unique additions to the wedding, such as the 360 photo booth and the musical selections performed. I had handpicked the songs to play as the guests arrived and during cocktail hour. We even had dances for both the bridal party and the groomsmen that I'd choreographed. Throughout the day, I was so excited, but I also felt like I was in a daze. One of my regrets was that I was not always in the moment that night despite being calm, cool, and collected. However, we'd done it, and I was now a married woman! Due to COVID-19 impacting travel so consistently during that time and us being unsure if we would be able to go where we desired in the Caribbean, we'd booked our honeymoon in Vegas.

I had lived by myself for five years up until the time of getting married, never once having a roommate. So, getting used to being engaged, transitioning to becoming husband and wife, and now living together was a huge adjustment. However, I began quickly adapting to all the transitions. I think one of the more challenging things earlier on was finding balance. On top of what I just mentioned, we'd also recently gotten a townhouse together and gone through the transition of packing up, leaving my apartment complex of five years, and relocating to the opposite side of town. However, I quickly adapted to change.

I was the quirky person who often celebrated certain dates, so for instance, as our one month of marriage approached, I was sure to acknowledge it. However, as the second month approached, my world as I knew it came crashing down. I learned that my husband of two months had been cheating on me. Even worse, he had been cheating even before we had gotten married *and* up until that point. I was devastated and instantly felt crushed. I did not know how to process what I was uncovering. As the weeks continued, more and more secrets about addiction and infidelity began to unfold. I was furious with him, and I was angry with myself! I thought, *Is this what I was unsure about the day before our wedding? How could I have not seen the signs? How was I fooled in this way?* We took the "right" steps. We had marriage mentors, we went through premarital counseling, we read books together, he told me all the right things, and he even spoke negatively about those who he knew were cheaters, so how could this be happening? Things got so bad that I felt like I was waking up to hell on earth for months, and only those close to me knew. I was losing so much of myself. I was fearful to leave due to things that had occurred during this time frame, but I also knew that staying was breaking me. The ugly sides of me began coming out due to the betrayal, my words became like venom from being hurt, and I had no clue how to move forward.

We'd signed up for marriage counseling, we'd connected back with our married mentors, we'd gone back to sessions with our pastor, we'd tried finding ways to reconnect, he'd joined addiction therapy, I'd started attending spousal addiction therapy to learn how to support him throughout this process, and the list went on. The unfortunate thing and the hard truth was that despite those who were in our corner rooting for us and supporting us both individually and as a couple, the lies did not stop. I found myself getting to a point where I just desperately wanted to hear the truth. I did not know what the truth was, and I often sought out to find it.

Truth is, I'd gotten to a point of being so broken down and emotionally distraught that our relationship felt beyond repair, and as I realized that I was never going to fully be able to let my guard down and trust him, I knew that it was time to leave. I had grown up seeing so many marriages around me, and due to my religious background, it was not something that I thought I would do. I was almost embarrassed by the thought of it because here I was, nine months after being married, filing for divorce. I worried about the wrong things, such as what people would think. Even amid my own tragedy, I was worried about exposing my truth and reality. I questioned myself and wondered if I was making the right decision. However, just as I'd questioned whether I should get married, I had that same uneasy feeling when it came to whether I should stay.

TRANSITION

In December of 2022, I filed for divorce. As the holidays approached, and as I had started the year initially thinking about the end of the year, I could not imagine that my first Christmas as a married woman would also be the same Christmas that I was alone. Though I had moved back in with my parents, the truth is, that is how I felt because I kept saying this was not how things were supposed to be. Even despite the period of the immense transition, I tried to keep an uplifted demeanor; I tried not to show that I was broken. One day, as I was having a conversation with my dad, he asked, "How are you doing, boo?" Boo was the nickname that he often referred to me by. I said, "I'm okay, Dad," trying my hardest to even form a half-cornered smile. As I began walking out the door, he grabbed my arm and pulled me in for a huge hug. Being in my dad's arms and feeling safe around a man that I could trust were what I needed. I rarely cried in front of my parents, and in that moment, I sat on my dad and sobbed and wept like a baby, exerting all my pain into my tears, so much so to the point that it made my dad cry. The same man whom I had only seen shed a few tears in my entire life was now also crying due to the pain that I felt. From that moment on, even as my dad thought that I was sleeping, I would feel a gentle touch on my forehead nearly every night as he would pray over me and anoint my head with holy oil.

The same went for my mom. One night, I sat downstairs curled up in a ball, and my mom heard me stuffy-nosed and crying despite trying to have the TV turned up so that no one could hear me. She ran downstairs, embraced me with a big hug, and let me know that I could do it and that the pain that I felt was only temporary. She immediately began praying over me as she rocked me in her arms. Little did my parents know that they were planting another seed at that moment when it came to pushing past obstacles. The truth is, you cannot do it by hoping or wishing it away; you must first start by having faith that you *will* surpass the storm. Matthew 17:20 NIV states, "Truly I tell you, if you have faith as small as a mustard seed, you can say to this mountain, 'Move from here to there,' and it will move. Nothing will be impossible for you." Even if I have not thanked them enough, or those who were in my corner uplifting me during this time, I am grateful.

Throughout the transition, I continued with my own therapy, and I learned that with divorce, you often also go through a grieving period because you ruminate on how you thought things were going to be. For a short period of time, I began slipping into a depression. I was exhausted all the time. I was numb, yet I felt sadness. I didn't have much of an appetite, and

I was wondering how I could ever get out of this hole.

You know, they say when you go through something, you really learn who your friends are. Let's just say that year was also the beginning of losing those who I thought were solid people in my life. However, I learned that when faced with adversity, it can often show you who's really in your corner. On the contrary, I am thankful because I also had a lot of support. One gift that I received after the holidays came from a childhood friend, and it was right on time as I was saddened by the fact that the new year was quickly approaching and I was entering it without my husband.

At this point, I'd grown to know that leaving was not something that I wanted to do, but it was necessary for me to do. So, to further explain, my heart was still in one place, but I had to start looking forward to where I was going as opposed to where I currently was. As I began to open the package, the gift that I'd received was a candle, card, and mug. The cup design was full of affirmations as well as scriptures, some of those being Mark 10:27, Phil 4:13, Ecclesiastes 3:11, and 2 Corinthians 12:9. As I looked up what each scripture referenced, it was a monumental moment because the scriptures began pouring life back into me. I started believing that maybe, just maybe, I could overcome this.

I was already part of an online fitness community at the time called Queen Warriors. The trainer was hosting an online women's conference called the It's Givin' Health, Wealth, and Healing Conference. The theme is in the name—it was an extremely special moment of women coming together to create change and impact. We discussed change and impact occurring naturally through health, but not only physical health—through emotional, financial, and spiritual health, as well. Throughout the conference, they spoke so much about mindset. This is crucial because what we think and feel about ourselves and what we allow to seep in can have a trickle effect on the physical, emotional, financial, and spiritual health areas in our lives. If the enemy can take hold of what you think about yourself, he will continue to keep that hold on you until you break free. When faced with adversity, you must begin speaking life into yourself. For example, saying affirmations—"I am strong," "I am beautiful," "I am worth it," "I am talented," "I am good enough"—and then pairing them with I will statements: "I will accomplish," "I will get through this," "I will win," "I will be successful," "I will achieve my goals."

When I was going through the transition, I not only did this on a consistent basis, but I also often would record myself. Though that may seem silly to some, I had to see myself speaking light into my current circumstances even on days when I felt that I didn't have the strength to do so. Sometimes, you must see it before you actually see it. When you're healing, you don't always just say, "Poof! I'm better." A lot of the time, it's an ongoing journey with conscious and intentional work put in to maneuver through that journey. Throughout the process, I would envision myself as whole and happy because I knew that life was not intended to be lived in bondage, and though I was not where I wanted to be quite yet, I knew that I would get there.

In Michigan, I grew up experiencing the four seasons. First, the snow and bitter cold of winter, which led to anticipating Groundhog Day to determine how close we were to the spring season. From there, I recall hearing, "April showers bring May flowers," as we maneuvered through spring and made it to summer. This then led to a drop in temperature and seeing the gorgeous color change in the leaves as we entered another season, fall. As I aged, I grew to develop an appreciation for the four seasons and the beauty in each one. Like seasons that are related to weather conditions, there are seasons related to life. Each season in your life may bring about something different than the season that you were previously in. Sometimes, you will have happy moments, and sometimes, you will experience hardships. However, as the aforementioned popular saying states, "April showers bring May flowers," such beauty can be found in seasonal transition. Embrace it.

HER LIGHT

CHAPTER 4

Working For More

When I was younger, I would often hear adults say that kids grow up so fast. As a teenager, I was also eager to experience adulthood in some shape or form, whether that was by making my own money, having my own place, or paying bills (Silly, right?) My mom used to always say, "Boo, don't be in a rush to grow up. Enjoy being a kid because you won't get this time back." Wasn't that the truth? Now in my late twenties, I often reminisce on the joys of being a child, such as not having to make tough decisions, having minimal responsibilities, not having to pay bills, and the list goes on. As I aged, the common phrase that we used amongst our friend group was, "Oh, I'm just adulting."

Growing up, my parents always taught me the value of working hard in all that you do. We lived a middle-class lifestyle and things were not always easy, but my parents always worked hard to provide for me and my brother. That consisted of them, at times, working two jobs and making sacrifices to afford a better life down the road. When I was a child, my dad made one of the most selfless decisions to go back to school. Not only was he a minister, but he also worked a full-time job, was a full-time student, and—obviously—was a parent. I remember my mom working second shift, so, my dad would bring me and my brother to the university in the hall outside the classroom, plug in the portable TV, and pop in a movie while he attended night classes.

Mmm, mmm, mmm, I was always excited to attend class with my dad because before heading to class, he'd pick up a nice, cheesy pepperoni and sausage pizza from a local favorite restaurant. Plus, the other students were always so nice to me and my brother. That was a sheer moment of my dad doing the best that he could with what he had. I don't recall my dad ever complaining about the busyness; instead, I believe he made it his mission to keep pushing despite the obstacles that were thrown his way up until graduation. Seeing his work ethic instilled something in me. As previously stated, ironically enough, I became the person in my late teens to early twenties working a full-time job, being a full-time student, and coaching.

My first job after college was working for a staffing company. I initially was looking for an opportunity to either become an admissions rep or a recruiter. In my interview with the staffing agency, the director who interviewed me had a different approach. He'd sized me up in the interview to better understand my values and character. He'd also peeled back many layers as I'd reciprocated the vulnerability that he'd shown. I felt that I'd really begun to get a glimpse of what the company was about from the interview based on how highly the director spoke about the company and what it represented. Up until that point, I hadn't seen someone see so much potential in me just from a conversation. From his words, I'd let him know that I wanted to be the Lebron James of the team—someone who was a team player and who would also work their butt off to become a top performer. You see, not only did my work ethic come from watching my dad work so hard as I grew up, but it also came from being the underdog in many areas in life that I'd become a "prove it" person. I thought about my life and how easily it could have been to have a pessimistic attitude; instead, my thought process was to change the narrative. I was going to prove it by showing up as an optimist and demonstrating that despite what obstacles are thrown your way, you have the ability to overcome them. I became so focused on self-development and improvement. I quickly excelled in my role, and one of the lessons that I'd learned early on is that often on your road to success, you can't do it all by yourself; you need to lean on other people for support. I began teaming up with those who were where I wanted to go. I would do things like schedule breakfast and lunch meetings with the account managers and establish consistent touch points with my manager and director, often seeking out feedback to better understand my opportunities for growth.

Throughout the early stages of my career, I knew that my goal was to get promoted to account manager. At that time, the organization focused on three buckets: production, business development, and servant leadership. When it came to production, that simply meant that you were performing. Business development during that time was based on the number of meetings with prospective clients that you could set as a recruiter, and what, if any business came from it. Servant leadership revolved around the mindset of bringing others with you. While recruiting, the production space came easy. I believe a portion of that was due to my heavy customer service background; I made a strong effort to build relationships with those whom I was recruiting and to find the best opportunities based on what they were looking for. I'd initially struggled with business development and servant leadership.

As my director saw that I was interested in advancing my career, he quickly took to investing in me. That revolved around speaking in rooms that I wasn't in, offering up opportunities with other leaders in the organization, and having consistent developmental meetings with me. One day, after having a developmental conversation and discussing my long-term goals, he gave me some tough feedback: For me to be great in my role,

I needed to give up my tendency of always wanting to be liked, as when I became a manager, I sometimes would have to make difficult decisions. He asked me if I'd heard of something called the EML triangle business motto. It was a leadership tool used to determine what kind of person you needed to be in the moment. E stood for Expert, M stood for Manager, and L stood for Leader. As we walked through examples of each, he informed me that he wanted me to begin sending a weekly report to him and my direct manager communicating how I'd acted as an expert, manager, or leader amongst my team. My initial thoughts were that it felt silly; why would my peers listen to me in this way? Though I had seen some success from a production standpoint, I hadn't even been with my company for a full year at that time. However, the power behind this exercise was that it caused me to be aware and make intentional strides at becoming an effective leader. I sent that report every week for fourteen months straight.

When it came to the business development side of things, after many rejections when attempting to set a meeting with a client, I eventually strengthened my craft. This, again, was thanks to my manager and director. The initial goal for prospective recruiters wanting to get promoted in my operation was to set one meeting per week; as I'd accomplished that, the next goal was to set two meetings per week. Next, it was to set two meetings per week, but now in my specific division with prospective clients. Then, it was to set two meetings a week, in my division, but they also needed to be in a set territory. I consistently felt the pressure due to learning that as I continued to hit goals, the bar increased. Within an eight-week time frame, I went from initially needing to set one meeting per week to having to set a total of seventeen. That was a moment that I was very proud of because as I'd eventually gotten promoted, I learned how to maneuver through the "no"s a bit easier.

The lesson here: How can you excel in life without being

pushed and tested? Oftentimes, it can become so easy to see where someone is and not know all that it took to get there. If you aren't tested in some shape or form throughout the journey, once you reach the level that you're targeting, will you fold when the bar is raised? That specific comment does not only pertain to work but to life in general. As I think about my work experience, I see that it was all preparing me to keep climbing. I am very fortunate for the fact that many of the leaders that I had believed in me, invested in me, and respected my decision even when it came time to transition to something else.

IT'S THE PRINCIPLE

My first job ever was working at a fast-food restaurant. This job taught me how to multitask. I took pride in what I did, and I always wanted to leave my stamp. I often tried to showcase my upbeat, cheerful voice through the drive-through and start up conversations with customers in the dining area. I excelled when it came to customer service, so much so to the point that I even had customers try to leave me tips on multiple occasions, though I could not accept them. Even when it was my turn to clean the bathrooms and mop the floors during the night shift, I did so with pride. I made sure that the bathrooms were spic and span, that the countertops shined, that the bottoms of the tables had no residue, that everything was fully stocked, and that there wasn't a crumb to be found in the dining space. My mindset was that in all things, do your best, and create a brand of what you want to represent.

My time here was very valuable because fast-forward to my account management role, I never shied away from talking to anyone, and I'd developed a true appreciation for what each member of a company did to make it run. To me, it didn't matter if you were the janitor or the CEO; I understood that every person played a vital role and to treat them as such. In my role as a teller, I'd heard about the opportunity from a customer while working in retail. They made a simple comment that they thought that I would make an excellent teller, and I eventually applied. When I first started at my location, the personal banker, assistant manager, and branch manager were all women. They were also all very good at what they did; it inspired me to want to do the same. On top of my daily teller responsibilities, I also had set goals pertaining to account recommendations as well as getting people to sign up for credit cards. Though I'd initially struggled, my assistant manager said something to me in 2013 that stayed with me throughout my career and up until this point. She said, "Brittany, sometimes you have to weed through a 'no' to get to a 'yes.'" How true is that? How often do we experience rejection and come to a standstill? If we gave up on all our goals just because people told us no, who would ever accomplish anything?

After my teller job, I also worked for a period as a leasing agent. I remember that one of my favorite aspects of the job was giving tours to prospective clients. I'd become excellent at painting pictures for them to help them envision what they could do with their space and get them thinking about things that they possibly hadn't thought about. The funny thing is, each experience that you have can set you up to prepare for something greater in the future. Little did I know that even my experiences here would carry on to my future jobs.

Most of my career has revolved, in some shape or form, around sales. One word that my coworkers often used to describe me was "extra." I was over the top in many things that I did, from my bold personality and pink decked-out office to even things such as going above and beyond when it came to my creativity in creating business reviews. One day, as I was going to a meeting with my manager, I pulled out a shiny bedazzled glitter business card holder that I had. I looked at her and instantly reflected on the "Brittany, you're extra" comments I'd gotten from others over the course of my career. Though now it may seem silly to think about how deeply I thought about things back then, I was still developing as a salesperson, and I often overthought the smallest things. I said, "Maybe I should get another card holder because maybe I am too extra." I also began worrying about my ability to connect with clients. In the meetings that I shadowed, I sometimes felt a bit intimidated. Growing up in the city that I was from, I'd often hear conversations in those meetings related to hunting or things like skiing, nature, or water activities in Michigan. Many of the things that were discussed were things that I had no experience with, and I worried if anyone would like me or see me as relatable. After speaking with my manager, she said, "Brittany, you don't have to be like anyone else to be likable. You will be great at your job just by being who you are." In that moment, my manager empowered me in ways that remained with me for years.

The obstacles that I experienced in my career caused me to become a pay-it-forward person whenever I got the opportunity to do so. The girl who was once so insecure and worried about what people thought about her would later become a girl who spoke about company improvement in rooms with executive leaders. I also spoke on a live virtual company call about being a woman and person of color in the workplace and empowered those who may second guess themselves and their capabilities. In hindsight, it all started with certain principles that I'd established for myself.

HER LIGHT

<u>PRINCIPLE ONE:</u>
<u>Start by building your own confidence</u>

For starters, to become the leader that I was destined to be, the process first began with building confidence by not being afraid to use my voice, whether that meant being vulnerable enough and owning my development by seeking out help or by speaking up in meeting settings. Whenever I felt the little butterflies in my stomach when I wanted to comment on something that I was too afraid to speak about, I took the opportunity to just go for it. Then, I continued that habit by ensuring that whenever I was in a meeting, I was intentional in always being a present, engaged, and active participant. I started by using my voice at least once during each meeting by asking a question, answering a question, or making a comment. This began building my own self-confidence because, for starters, you never know who might be thinking the same thing as you but are too timid to share. By becoming more confident when it came to using my voice, I was propelled to partner with my coworkers and encourage them to do the same.

<u>PRINCIPLE TWO:</u>
<u>Be authentic and genuine in all that you do</u>

Share your goals and ambitions with leaders whom you trust in the workplace, get to know them on a personal level, and make consistent touch points with those who can become an advocate for you. By being yourself, you allow others to see the real you and speak in rooms that you're not in about your character. This means that if you are in a vulnerable state, don't be afraid to let people in sometimes. I used to think that if I cried or opened up to someone, allowing them to see any other emotion outside of happiness, people would label me as emotional. The reality is that people connect with individuals who are relatable, not perfect. You don't always have to be polished in everything that you say or do; you just have to show up and put your best foot forward. I eventually understood that it takes a lot of courage to be vulnerable with others, that is not a weakness but a strength. Also, I realized that if I was going to be successful one day, I wanted to do it by being exactly who I was. I didn't want to conform to being someone who I thought people would like; instead, I started to find value in who I was and what I could bring to the table by simply being me. I encourage you to do the same.

PRINCIPLE THREE:
Be the change that you want to see

For me, an area of focus that I've always been passionate about is having representation. If you feel that there's not enough representation in the field that you're in or future roles that you want to step into, become that change. When I was working on getting promoted, I wanted to give up many times. I felt that I was being tested and pushed too hard, and the journey felt so long. I then had an eye-opening moment one day and thought about what it would mean to the next person of color— how would it make them feel to step into the room and see someone who looks like them in that role? What would it cause them to think? Would they think, *If she did it, maybe I can do it too?* In that moment, that's when I knew that I had to keep going. That's when I realized that it was bigger than me—and to take it one step further for those reading this, it's also bigger than you. You don't know the people whom you'll impact or the change that you'll make, but the story is already written for you. You just have to take the steps and reach your potential because you're already destined for great things; you just have to believe in yourself. Start speaking light into yourself and drown out the negative noise.

ON TO NEW THINGS

After much reflection, and as I made the decision to depart from my first job after graduation and the company that I'd grown so much at over the years, I was initially very reluctant. I'd finally built up a name for myself, and I was so proud of what I'd accomplished. My job became part of my identity. As I drafted my resignation letter, I did so teary-eyed. It was because it was not something that I wanted to do; however, it was necessary in order for me to go in the direction that I was meant to go in the next season of my life.

It can become so easy to connect your self-worth to achievement and where you are at a certain stage in your life. However, I'd realized that what God had placed inside of me was not something that anyone could take away. My job gave me the tools for success, but it's not what made me successful or special. My ambition, work ethic, mindset, and character are what got me there. Evaluate what you bring to the table, and carry those characteristics with you. You don't have to fear change; you will shine wherever you go because it's already in you.

Now, in reading this section of the book, by no means am I telling you to quit your job. Instead, I want to empower you to understand your value, see the good in who you are, and be open to change. Perhaps that even means switching departments at work and trying something new. Or going for that promotion. Whatever it is, don't allow fear to blur your vision. Take risks, even if you do so while afraid.

CHAPTER 5

Everything's Bigger In Texas

My brother moved to Houston, Texas, right after I graduated from high school. Every time I visited him, it somehow felt like a calling. I always knew that Houston was where I eventually wanted to be. I'd attempted to move there twice with two different friends; I'd visited colleges there and envisioned my life there on multiple occasions. It was not until I was going through my divorce that I mustered up the courage to take a leap of faith. In a three-week time frame, I'd prayed and made up my mind that this time around, I was going to do it. Within three months of initially making the decision, I relocated to Houston. This decision did not come as a surprise to those who'd truly known me because I'd talked about it for nearly a decade, and I was proud of the fact that I'd finally done it.

When it came to the weeks leading up to the move, I was terrified. The thought of leaving my family, friends, and job to start over in an unknown territory was beyond scary. However, I'm grateful for taking a leap of faith and moving forward with the path that God had aligned for me. Despite how fear continued to creep in, I kept reminding myself that God's got me, and no matter what happened, I'd be okay. The day before the move, I packed up only what would fit in my SUV, and my parents drove me and my dog to Houston. As we crossed the Texas line, I exhaled a sigh of relief. Here I was, doing something that

47

I'd dreamt of for years! It goes to show that no matter how bad things get in life, or whatever bumps in the road you experience, it's never too late to start over. Now, that doesn't always mean that you must physically move. However, the word *move* is what's most important in that sentence. Oftentimes, we allow our circumstances to keep us stuck. Maybe that means settling into a job that you're miserable at, remaining in a friendship that no longer serves you, or depriving yourself of the beauty life can offer. I encourage you to live, take risks, and experience what's out there.

I always recalled hearing that everything is bigger in Texas. It was not until I moved that I learned that those who said that must have been referring to the bugs. I'm just kidding—but seriously, though. The insects are on another level, literally. Then, don't even get me started on the heat and traffic. I'd like to say that this chapter talks about nothing other than how happy I was after my move. However, it doesn't. After the move was when the real work began. The thing that most people don't talk about after maneuvering through life after hardship is just that: maneuvering through life afterward. I feel that a beautiful rainbow is often painted as opposed to really sharing some of the downfalls that were experienced. Back home, I'd built a name for myself. I was involved in my church, I knew many people in the cheer industry from my years of coaching, and I'd begun becoming established at work. I was a social butterfly, and to go from where I was known and comfortable to being in a place where I didn't know many people at all was an extremely hard adjustment.

I've always been someone who has a hard time sitting still; I was always active growing up and involved in something. When it came to safety, I kept hearing about the dangers of being a single woman in Houston, so I took my caution to the extreme. My first three to six months of moving, I spent quite a bit of time alone and confined to the four walls of my apartment due to the fear of enjoying the big city primarily alone. Oftentimes, people don't talk about the isolation period that you go through when you relocate, nor do they talk about just getting used to cultural adjustments. For me, driving from Grand Rapids, Michigan, to Muskegon, Michigan, felt like a decent commute that would not be made on a consistent basis. Well, news flash: In Houston, it's very common to commute forty to fifty minutes to most places that you go. Not only that, but it also felt like Houston was a completely foreign land. I'd started hearing of music genres that I'd never heard of before, such as Zydeco music. I'd also realized how obvious it was that I wasn't a Houston native due to certain vocabulary that I'd used. For instance, if I ever were to use the word "pop," I'd be corrected and informed that it's called "soda." On the contrary, I began learning about the true meaning behind Mardi Gras, exploring and enjoying authentic Cajun food, becoming accustomed to Houstonian culture, and enjoying the big, beautiful city. It was not until I finally started putting myself out there and embracing the change that I began to find enjoyment in this new foreign land.

As I stated previously, the true work began when I relocated. The work that I'm referring to is healing. I'd chosen me and picked myself up after my divorce, which is something that I will always be proud of. However, there was a great deal of healing that still needed to come from that. In my community, therapy was often looked down upon. However, that was where I started. I underwent EMDR (eye movement desensitization and reprocessing) therapy to target and focus on the areas of trauma in my life that I'd recently experienced as well as long past experiences that I'd never healed from. I got more active in church; however, this time around, it was more than just attending church. My prayer life increased, I started tithing, and I also focused on developing a true relationship with God. I began focusing on my health and fitness, and instead of continuing with crash diets, I was trying to create a healthy, enjoyable long-term lifestyle. I also worked heavily on self-development by reading books and starting many mornings listening to audiobooks, sermons, or podcasts. When you reach the point of trying to elevate in certain areas of your life, the analogy that I think of is once living as a caterpillar and transitioning to a butterfly. The species will undergo metamorphosis, and each stage is essential and serves a different purpose. When you relate that to your own life, everything that you've gone through is shaping you and preparing you for something greater. It's not until you break free from the cocoon and what's limiting you that you blossom as the beautiful butterfly that you are meant to be.

LESSON ONE:
Heal from the past

In college, I took many online classes, and one of my biggest regrets was taking several mathematics and upper-level courses online. I remember the constant fear and anxiety that I'd experienced because I often thought that I'd overlooked an assignment due on Blackboard or that I'd missed some deadline. We often had many tests to take, which had to be completed within a certain period. As a test concluded, you'd have access to review your score and reflect on what you got right and what you got wrong. From there, it was up to you to apply what you'd learned as you moved on to the next chapter and prepared for the next test.

That same concept is true in life. No matter what you do, you can't avoid being tested. That statement is not made in a pessimistic way; it's reality. You will consistently be tested in some shape or form, whether that's on the job, in school, with family, friendships, relationships, finances, even the way that you feel about yourself and your own self-worth. The trick here is using your experiences and learning from them. The experiences that you have can often initially feel like a setback; however, they can be the greatest setup towards a prosperous future if you allow them. The first step for me after I'd gotten past the reality of what all just occurred in my marriage was turning the mirror to myself—not necessarily in a way that I began blaming myself for everything that occurred, but in a way that I began to see the areas of myself that I had yet to heal from.

About six months after I'd moved, I felt a heaviness in my heart. Not once did I think that making the move was a mistake; I knew that I was where I was supposed to be. However, my heart felt hardened because I didn't get there how I'd initially thought I would. As I mentioned earlier, it was no surprise to those who truly knew me that I'd eventually end up in Texas; I'd talked about wanting to relocate for quite some time. Five months before my relocation, a former boss of mine who had moved several years ago actually told me about a job that the company she was working at was hiring for. She'd known about my interest in the DEI (diversity, equity, and inclusion) field, and sure enough, a position opened in Houston, Texas. As I'd talked to my then-husband about it, we'd decided that moving was not right. As our marriage drastically continued to decline, the irony was that I eventually ended up moving there anyway. However, I did not get there how I'd initially envisioned.

I pondered on that thought as I was in my kitchen cooking dinner. The heaviness began to feel overwhelming because as I looked around at my surroundings, I felt extremely blessed to now be living in a beautiful apartment community, but I also remembered that just one year prior to that, I was in Michigan and married. Not once did I foresee the way that my life at that moment came to be. The television played in the background, and

Tyler Perry was speaking about forgiveness. Ironically enough, he was speaking at Joel Osteen's church, who is a pastor in Houston, Texas. He said, "Forgiveness is not for the other person. It's for you." Though I had physically moved, and though I emotionally no longer had interest in my ex-husband, I realized that the heaviness I'd felt was because I had not forgiven him.

I paused what I was doing and began praying. I was harboring all these negative feelings and living in the past, holding on to things that I could not change. I no longer wanted to be that person who carried pain and negative energy; I wanted to break free from what had hardened my heart. It started with forgiveness. Though it was not healthy to call up my ex, I knew that I needed to release the anger that I had toward him. The moment that I knew it was still hurting me was when I tried to formulate the words and tears began pouring down my cheeks. Not only did I eventually release what I had to say into the atmosphere, I even said a prayer for him. I wished goodness in his life, that he would find happiness, and that he would also heal in the areas of his life that needed healing. In that moment, a weight lifted off my shoulders, and I felt like I could finally exhale.

LESSON TWO:
You can't please everyone

Coming to the realization that no matter what you do, you will be judged and criticized by somebody was an eye-opening experience for me. Others may say, "You'll always have haters," or, "Someone will always pray on your downfall." Now, ain't that the truth? For years, I spent so much time concerned about what others thought about me that I'd limited my own potential based on fear of being disliked, letting someone down, or going against popular opinions. I think about times in my life, particularly while coaching, when I wish I'd had the guts to worry less about what people thought of me. I would have made a way better coach by limiting and tuning out parents and giving up wanting to be liked and validated by my athletes. However, lessons learned.

That was not the only area that I was a people pleaser; it was in nearly every other area of my life. Throughout the journey of healing and self-discovery, I shifted this area in my life by doing the following:

Number One: Become less concerned with what people think and more concerned with true happiness and elevating your life. I got so focused on myself, and not in an arrogant way, but in a way that I wanted to improve in all areas. I knew that if I continued to listen to naysayers in every single area of my life, I'd never truly reach my potential. Instead, I began praying about things as well as only sharing what was necessary and with those whom I trusted.

Number Two: Don't be afraid to say no. As a matter of fact, let's practice it: *Nnnn...ooooo*. Putting up boundaries and not being so easily swayed and open to bending over backward for people is essential, especially when it's to your own detriment.

Number Three: Don't be afraid to stand on things. If you know you feel strongly about something, don't allow other people's opinions to alter your beliefs. Speak on it, even if that means standing alone in your viewpoints. I don't care if you bring something up in a work setting and you're the only one who believes in it. If you're confident in the thought and vision, don't allow other people to minimize your voice.

<u>Number Four</u>: Let go of what no longer serves you. I'd reached a point of realizing that many people were in my life due to longevity as opposed to value being added. When you're going to the next level, everyone can't go with you. When you really start ridding yourself of a people-pleasing mindset, you'll realize characteristics not only in yourself but in others, as well. Look at your circle. Are the people surrounding you individuals who have similar characteristics? Is the relationship one-sided? Are they equally supportive? Begin to evaluate those whom you surround yourself with.

<u>Number Five</u>: Protect your peace. When you move away from being a people pleaser, you may create friction with those around you. People may be surprised when you finally start saying no or putting up boundaries. That's okay; those who truly support you will respect and encourage the growth that's taking place in you. Don't feel bad about finally starting to think of yourself just as much as you think of other people.

LESSON THREE:
<u>Drown out the self-doubt and negativity</u>

When you are growing and developing, it will be so easy to go back to old mindsets, habits, and where you are comfortable because you're not used to change. I encourage you to embrace the change and tone down the noise. Throughout the process, be careful of what's being sown into you and what you share with people in general, especially during the healing journey because you need to be cautious as to what you're feeding into during vulnerable states.

Understanding your self-worth and value is something that you must work on internally. However, as you work on it, ensure that those who are in your corner speak light into you and encourage you to keep pressing on. Anytime I began to doubt myself, I would read my favorite scriptures, starting with Psalm 46:5 (NIV): "God is within her; she will not fall." This tells me that wherever I go and whatever I may experience, He is with me and guiding me along the way. Proverbs 31:25 (NKJV), "Strength and honor *are* her clothing; She shall rejoice in time to come," helps me to realize that I don't have to be ashamed of the past or afraid of the future. I can lift my head because I know that God has given me strength and that everything will be all right. Lastly, Romans 8:28 (NIV), "And we know that in all things God works for the good of those who love Him, who have been called according to His purpose," taught me that no matter what happens, all things are working together for something bigger and better than I could even imagine because that's the kind of God I serve.

I would also often recall the voice of my mom saying, "You can do it, baby girl." To me, maybe that meant writing a book, going for the promotion, or moving across the country. Her statement served as a gentle reminder to keep pushing. The fact of the matter is that I'd often experienced self-limiting beliefs, and it was necessary to correct my mindset. Sometimes, your inner critic can speak so loudly and tell you things like, "You're not good enough," "You're not talented enough," "You can't do it." Don't feed into those thoughts. I was usually the person who could pour into others, but I let the negative noise stop me from pouring into myself. I knew that I needed to show myself grace and speak light into who I was. Even before my divorce and the affirmations that I'd say during that stage of my life, I'd gotten to a point of saying occasional affirmations in the car as I drove to work. They went like this: "Girl, you are powerful. You're deserving of good things. You're capable. You're an overcomer. You're good enough." Start challenging yourself and your way of thinking because oftentimes, it's your mindset that will hold you back.

I'd reached a knowing and realization that when it comes to truly identifying your purpose and living the life God has set out for you, it will require a true encounter with God. An encounter in which you can't rely on anyone else but Him. A time when your faith is truly tested, but that mustard seed keeps you moving. You don't know how your light, your achievement, and your ability to overcome just might be tied to the success of others. I often think about some of the people whom I admire and look up to the most. Firstly, my parents, as well as known celebrities such as Steve Harvey, Jamie Kern Lima, Oprah Winfrey, and LeBron James. I think about how others may have been impacted if those individuals decided to give up on their goals and dreams when tragedy and hardships hit. It's bigger than you. Keep going.

CHAPTER 6

Be The Light

As I've shared a glimpse of my life, it was not written to boast about anything, nor as a self-pity party. I pray that the choices I made when it came to choosing worthiness, choosing becoming whole, and choosing to still love others despite hardship can serve as an inspiration. Allow this section of the book to serve as the opportunity to let go of what you can't control and to forgive those who have harmed you. We live in a world of imperfect people; not one person has lived a life without mistakes, regrets, or hardships. Break free from what is heavy in your heart, and maneuver toward becoming the person you're set out to be.

One of my favorite classes in college was my interpersonal communications course. I took this course over ten years ago, and I still remember one particular assignment like it was yesterday. Our professor instructed us to have what she called a "no complaining day" and to write a paper on it. When you slow down and are cautious of what you complain about, it really causes you to have a humble heart and to appreciate what you have and what's around you. I've included a few lines below; if you can, try it out. Reflect on your day and write down every moment when you felt yourself dwelling on something or getting upset. Also, please include why it upset you and your reaction after the situation.

HER LIGHT

Now that you've done that, think about it. Was getting upset with the person who cut you off in traffic worth it? Or letting what someone said weigh you down? Often, it wasn't. That assignment helped me shift my perspective in moments of anger and frustration to something more powerful: acceptance. It also helped me learn to not allow certain circumstances to negatively impact the energy that I give off to the world. You can't go back in the past and change what may have occurred; however, you can decide how you choose to respond to it.

SHINING YOUR LIGHT

"Our deepest fear is not that we are inadequate. Our deepest fear is that we are powerful beyond measure. It is our light, not our darkness, that most frightens us. We ask ourselves, 'Who am I to be brilliant, gorgeous, talented, fabulous?' Actually, who are you not to be? You are a child of God. Your playing small does not serve the world. There is nothing enlightened about shrinking so that other people won't feel insecure around you. We are all meant to shine, as children do. We were born to make manifest the glory of God that is within us. It's not just in some of us; it's in everyone. And as we let our own light shine, we unconsciously give other people permission to do the same. As we are liberated from our own fear, our presence automatically liberates others."

— Marianne Williamson

Growing up in church, one of the first songs that I recall learning is "This Little Light of Mine." For me, that song served to tell me that wherever you go, find a way to shine so brightly and use the God-given light in all that you do. This is also reflected in Matthew 5:16 NKJV, which states, "Let your light so shine before men, that they may see your good works and glorify your Father in heaven."

When it comes to being a beacon of light, I have a couple of areas for you to focus on.

<u>Number One:</u> Prioritize self-love.

Hopefully, I was able to paint a picture of healing in the last chapter. A portion of that healing also involves loving yourself. You don't have to be like anyone else, you don't have to talk like anyone else, and you certainly don't have to dress like anyone else. Appreciate what makes you who you are, it's your uniqueness that makes you special. As you grow to love yourself and as you become confident in who you are, this will become a step toward allowing your light to shine without limitations.

<u>Number Two</u>: How can you be a light in this world?

For starters, it can be as simple as greeting everyone at work each day, taking the time to help someone in need, or showing kindness to a stranger. Shining your light does not always have to involve money; it just involves you making a conscious, intentional effort. One of my favorite quotes comes from the famous poet and activist, Maya Angelou. She states, "I've learned that people will forget what you said, people will forget what you did, but people will never forget how you made them feel."

As you work on identifying and shining your light, I challenge you to think about this: What kind of person do you want to be in this world? How will you make others feel? How will you exist? How will you show up? As I was writing this book, it was important to me to highlight pivotal moments thus far. Many of those moments were painful. However, throughout the journey, I realized that what caused a great deal of hurt ended up being what I called painful blessings. Something that could have been used to allow for excuses or a negative outcome was used to increase my faith and allow me to maneuver toward the person I was destined to become. You see, we can't choose our story; it's unique and special to us. However, what you can choose is how you decide to respond to it.

Everybody has a story, and the journey toward becoming the best version of yourself and walking in your purpose is not always an easy path. Along the way, you will be tested, and it will seem like going back to your old ways and back to who you were will be far easier than stepping into who you're becoming. Choose to evolve, choose to continue taking up space in this world, and choose to be a light. May your light never be dimmed by naysayers or self-doubt. Instead, allow it to shine so brightly that it gives others hope and inspires them to do the same.

With Love,
Brittany

HER LIGHT